Theme of the Parabola

ALSO BY IAN RANDALL WILSON

Hunger and Other Stories

THEME OF THE PARABOLA

A Chapbook

Ian Randall Wilson

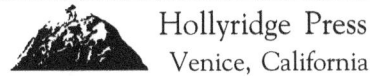

Hollyridge Press
Venice, California

© 2005 Ian Randall Wilson

All rights reserved under International and Pan-American Copyright Conventions. Published in the United States by Hollyridge Press.

Hollyridge Press
P.O. Box 2872
Venice, California 90294
www.hollyridgepress.com

Cover Design by Rio Smyth
Manufactured in the United States of America by Lightning Source

ISBN-13: 978-0-9752573-3-3
ISBN-10: 0-9752573-3-1

Grateful acknowledgment is made to the editors of the following publications where these poems first appeared:

5_Trope: "A Question For The Romantic Lap"; "The Optional of Obvious"
Aught: "A Lack of Correspondence to the Familial World"; "An Illustrated Text Aimed at Engineers"; "Dear It"; "Empire"
BlazeVox2k2: "Forget Everything You Thought You Knew About Slip Covers"; "Learning From Lumpiness"; "Life"
Forklift: "The Museum of Stammers"
Gestalten: "The Golden Age of Peanut Butter"
Incliner: "Little Red Neighborhood"
La Petite Zine: "Translations From Languor Not Yet Spoken"
Opium Magazine: "Why Not Get A Puppy?"
Puerto Del Sol: "The Jar Overflowing With Emptiness"
Score: "These are Words Estranged in a Row"
Sugar Mule: "The Injured, The Admired"; "The Decay Of Probability"
Tin Luster Mobile: "I Gloss the History of the Human Tongue"
Vert: "The Ballad of Sad Curtain"; "Theme of the Parabola"
WordForWord: "Everything I Say Has The Ring Of Untruth"
www.muse-apprentice-guild.com: "Sheep Weep"

12 11 10 09 08 07 06 05   10 9 8 7 6 5 4 3 2 1

Contents

The Decay Of Probability	3
Empire	5
Theme of the Parabola	7
A Lack of Correspondence to the Familial World	9
Forget Everything You Thought You Knew About Slip Covers	10
Life	14
Everything I Say Has The Ring Of Untruth	17
Learning From Lumpiness	19
The Injured, The Admired	20
Why Not Get A Puppy?	21
These are Words Estranged in a Row	22
Little Red Neighborhood	23
The Museum of Stammers	24
The Jar Overflowing With Emptiness	26
I Gloss the History of the Human Tongue	27
Dear It	28
A Question For The Romantic Lap	29
The Optional of Obvious	30
The Ballad of Sad Curtain	31
Translations From Languor Not Yet Spoken	33
An Illustrated Text Aimed at Engineers	34
The Golden Age of Peanut Butter	36
Sheep Weep	37

Theme of the Parabola

THE DECAY OF PROBABILITY

The first level of knowledge
in order to write the "great
poem" is to characterize its properties,
the next, the information
needed to specify a position
in a given accuracy.
Sometimes poets using these methods
spend their days plotting
data, drawing little boxes
and counting the number
of data points in each box.
Crude, yes, but for the first
time chaos is within reach
of poetic systems.
They look for poems
in flapping flags
and rattling speedometers,
searching out chaos in the
current literature.
Unexplained noise, surprising
fluctuations, regularity mixing
with irregularity—these effects
pop up in poems from
experimentalists working with everything from
pantoum accelerators to laser sonnets.
Several experiments on josephson junction octa
rima reveal a striking noise-rise
phenomena in audiences.
But the collective is a problem—
one partner for a clean job,
the tendency toward crate mixing.

In the end, I can only conclude
the brothels of poetry are
manned by crippled pimps—
Hot doggy, I always
wanted to say that
or something like it.

EMPIRE

We are a complex us
living in air the color
of deviance forgetting others.
Dusk holds in the rhythmic earth
everything name and lacking content,
flame it must.
From the clamor I extract a national blue,
a land something, unconsciousness under capes,
a modicum of if.
From the grove an extended son and no promised end,
the world body erased
its coated form thrown careless.

I mucked about in a deity haze surrounded by confusing
spirit guides, a ceremonial do-wop dawn.
I was one of the coat common watching my silhouette.
I worked to separate the beautiful from the dusty out here
by the river of funny beneath an idiot night.

In the human archaic mirror,
our intellect, our hallucinatory naught—
it recalled it, the disheveled much.
Time to feast again on dull aspirin,
leave kind do nobody and wait
like brewers' children for the casual end.

Me Kansas, you Jane.
My head is an empty summary,
my present suffers from a case of cat owner's lap.
Nothing tears great things.
Now past story I'm writing of somehow, thinking
of some way, planning for something
as rain ignites disinterest.

Some gifts are tractors
the blue be
and oil of small charity.
With a distinct lack
of the visionary it,
the visionary here,
the visionary why,
we watch out for a doll burst,
come camp wonderful,
we give each other the psychiatrist's clasp
then exchange bright ferns.
What are a few decibels among friends
working back from the laughter formula to a city system
to my home my America where language falls dark.

THEME OF THE PARABOLA

some nights a voice in my hand won't shut up
some nights are another oasis decayed
some nights I acquire books
some nights I am a jazz buff
some nights I am the giant Escondido
some nights I am wonderfully advanced
some nights I count one time at a time
some nights I don't think of the girl in the next work
 cubicle
some nights I fall in love with things from 35 five years
 ago, but that stuff's not being done anymore and no
 one talks that way
some nights I get a voice
some nights I give interest
some nights I lose a voice
some nights I blame everyone as a strategy for world
 domination
some nights I receive a plaque as employee of the month
some nights I sort piles into neat bones
some nights I think about Communism and love poetry
some nights I wear a cuff with the proper break and the
 acid reflux on a brand new bed, the second car cooling
 outside and inside I wish for central air-conditioning
 and the Pulitzer Prize, a cabin on the lake and the
 Steve signal from the Beloved
some nights in that wonderful oak nightstand in my chest
 full of old pictures and credit cards out of date the
 Beloved and I spend time exchanging mulch
some nights life progresses and the new house is better
 than the old
some nights my music is the extended rest note
some nights the Beloved agrees
some nights the Beloved uses her hips

some nights the cats attack my toes
some nights the cats sleep
some nights the ceiling fan rumbles
some nights the death of better
some nights the lights outside become lovely
some nights the scar on my back doesn't throb
some nights the windows fog
some nights the word is dangerous and needs to be left alone
some nights the world is left over roast cooling on a plate
some nights there's paper but the wrong light
some nights want is left surface
some nights we are busy work

A LACK OF CORRESPONDENCE TO THE FAMILIAL WORLD

Perhaps I'm misspelling.
Perhaps I'm guilty
of present-tense vandalism
or dumb to the proper settings
of poetic space heaters.
To get the point across
the weaker of us lean
on the defaults: smoke
and mirror mannerisms labeled three,
fake dream drawings,
full-spectrum pronouns.
Don't hit me with
your speech act theory, man,
your dark mountain couplings,
your language barriers
because that jumbo don't work on me.
There's too many in here
for me to keep track
and I'm not even sure
of my own self.
But let me misquote Ted:
It's not a little exciting
to keep a sponge
in your back pocket
and it's not a little silly,
too, it's what's happening
in California and the rest
of the world at the start of 2002.

FORGET EVERYTHING YOU THOUGHT YOU KNEW ABOUT SLIP COVERS

No one ordered the chaos research to stop
it just did the way we hope—all right —
the way I hope for sex on Sunday
and it doesn't happen.
The dripping faucet has certain advantages.
One important variable is the rate of flow,
the surface tension.
Nature favors just a few— the rest must expand
the human breast beyond the limits
of all expectations.
Could an expert in chaotic dynamics
find something useful to say?
Can my father if polled?
Any me?
Me?

I imagine a weight hanging from a string.
I image the weight grows with time.
Poor string.
Only three equations are necessary for chaos
but at least four occasions are required.
This is one of them as I demonstrate
myself efficient at bringing noise
from the little league scales
to the big league scales.
I'm telling you I'm hard
up and full of loopy
trails of smoke left
by a sky-writing plane.
The structure was unmistakable
and I'll spend
the next few days consuming myself.

It would be enough, I suppose, to speak of thermal
transducers, Lorentz attractors and the dripping faucet
while the whole group attended the second chaos meeting.
Put aside everything you think you know
about paradigm shifts
and prepare for the ninety-fifth dimension,
prepare for a world without a unionized god,
prepare for a time without the penis,
then occupy the single point you're passing
through right NOW
for as long as you have left.
Consider the shelf life of facts
how much less there is to know
when there's nothing to know.
Consider the knowledge of rocks
then find a typewriter.
Do not be shy.
Do not leave papers beneath people's doors
and for god's sake don't leave the secret
plans for saving the king on the counter
of some god damn ski shop in Utah.
Say difference say stranger say chewing
thought and swallow
then take another bite.
Do not be shy.
The collective cannot go on forever.

Time for me to confront the controlled it,
the it which knows
and has warm opinions of the earliest fashion.
Now I'll take my doorstep mind into the
joke corner for another round
with the unintelligible it, the charming it, the scion it, the formless
it, the it that found fame in the Northwest Passage, the hill it, the
mountain it, the it of the universal divide, it feels, it sees, it sits

high, it can't know, it is of limited vision, it experiences dissatisfaction, it loves the hand, it writes from the heart because its grandmother died—recently—the it word here on the beach, the light outrageous, later is best when catastrophe sides with Armageddon to produce a new sugar-free dessert.
Important to question the not.
It likes it fast.
See it, hear it, smell it.
Go ahead and touch it.
Okay, please?
That's it
now taste it.
Possible?
Im-possible?
Enjoy it.

Today's swamp is just ending,
don't mind me thinking radio,
don't mind me thinking.
Attention to things becomes attention to language
then the thing itself slips from view,
a style of profusion again nothing
again different again celibate.
We don't pick our lives:
i.e., no running romance up the flagpole
to ask if the will, the it of the it,
is necessarily colored
by prevailing contradictions.
Is rain predicted?
I don't expect
names cut across echoes.
There's a lot of hours left in the day
and with a moored mind and unmoored body
I'm trying once more to arrange the marriage of Heaven
with anything else.
I keep on seeding the night

when the future is floors and I don't
know exactly what I want
or when I might get it.
Ideas anyone?
Good.

LIFE

Before attempting to analyze
let me note how
it makes noises like meaning,
points in the direction of meaning
(a small town in Cote d'Alene, OR),
gives up the ghost of meaning,
carries with it—though neatly tucked
in a breast pocket—the shadow
of meaning, then, from the woodpile
out back comes the lingering
smell of meaning, and along
the baseboards and by
the shores the residue of meaning
like in the forest behind
my father's house once
the track of meaning (though
all that remains are the rail beds
and cinders and a few loose nails),
the basic unit of meaning which is around
a buck fifty (in 1990 dollars), suffocated
by meaning but that is a whole other discussion,
a world of meaning not to be confused
with the universe of meaning something equally
different than the transgalactic conduit
of possible meaning—and I could go on
into other dimensions in the name
of supreme meaning because
I believe if you shout long enough
and loud enough you may be rewarded with
the echoes of meaning, of course
scribbled hastily on the backs
of check stubs and race
programs for losers the meaning of outline

which is a step away or forward or back from the structure of meaning, the unintended meaning, the paraphrase and parabola of meaning, the connections of meaning, the hyperbola of meaning, the passage of meaning, the extended meaning, how it has the appearance of meaninglessness but must mean, must explore the very conditions of meaning, show new ways of meaning (and new ways means new roads and new houses, many more people, one or two decent restaurants, a movie theatre, the inevitable strip mall—even if of meaning not a good thing), a season of meaning, the exhortation of meaning though I am not a prayerful man (perhaps I meant exultation but I am often confused), the sedimentary meaning which requires careful excavation but in the laying of such foundations we're back to all that building and the damn strip mall, the laceration of meaning, the implication, imbrications (or did I mean imprecations), and insinuation of meaning, resonating with meaning the way the crystal wine glass shrieks as it pleads for sexual release, and damn me if I haven't forgotten the elusive hidden meaning just back from vacationing on the coast, the meaning that resists young starlets and other delusions of grandeur, the irreducible meaning never good for sauces because it does not get thick, the order of meaning and his Boswell the meaning of order, the rejection of meaning which is no worse than the loss of any lover unless it is for the first time, believe me, that hurts, the reflexive meaning which salutes without thinking (and we're seeing a lot of that in 2002), which walks to the right on every set of stairs, which insists on meat, nothing but meat—and potatoes—with each meal, the self-conscious meaning always difficult to dress, the inspirational meaning—trust me, you do not want me to sing, the parodic meaning a distant cousin of sporadic meaning but funnier, the meditative meaning fine for those of us not on a budget or schedule, with a car in the shop and the rent due and the marriage in trouble a sure sign of partial meaning, divergent meaning, the loss of meaning which produces pure sadness and down the block the disjunctive meaning, the subjunctive meaning, the subjective meaning, party guests we shall try to avoid, the collapsing meaning, the collaborative meaning, the conducive meaning, the constructive meaning (weary, weary, I grow weary), the pre-

carious meaning, the involuted meaning, the vacuum-packed meaning which comes in its own stay-fresh pouch and is good for years, the revelatory meaning, the hierarchical meaning, the appropriate meaning which varies from state to state, the uncertain meaning and its negation that certain meaning, the anecdotal meaning which—disconnected as I am from my self, I almost forgot, the constant meaning, the centripetal meaning, the typical meaning, the archetypal meaning, the abiding meaning shacked up with the abiding image though they have given up drink, the sympathetic meaning, syntactic meaning, the grasping strangling vaguely sexual paraphrasable meaning, the performative meaning (and I see we're still on sex), the long long long search for meaning among trees, among people of another tribe, among flora, among foreigners (I've repeated myself, sorry), and all the presuppositions—a very long word of what meaning I was never sure—of meaning which often leads to faux meaning, forced meaning not to be confused with forced labor or false labor (quite a pain), and the beauty of innuendo which at this point demands a call for clarity which is meaning at its finest, the repudiation of meaning—one trolley stop in the path of enlightenment that brings about new meaning, the bridging of meaning, the well-intentioned meaning, the master meaning, yes, the master,
the meaning behind
the meaning and the meaning of meaning
and let us not ignore
the haiku of meaning
for which I drop
this stone
here.

EVERYTHING I SAY HAS THE RING OF UNTRUTH

On our way past nothingness
we carried caviar on our backs.
We spent days appreciating hiccups.
We had slogans, music birds, reviews.
The sins of our fathers
was our dying paradigm.
We used blades to
look for help
permanently scarred ourselves.
We translated son and it became
the century, cloud for diplomats,
gloves like crucibles of iron, new
underclothes of the berries. Useless
to say our dictionaries were fouled,
communication inconclusive—
the same moment bounced elsewhere
the same shadow jugging you
the same excuse snowmen used
the same road almost melon
the same sadness deflowered
the same maelstrom
the same eddy, the vortex, whirl, arm of the turn,
    commotion, fury, storm
the same turmoil fighting idea
the same acetate trick love
the same big arm story
the same love song an exercise in mouth metrics
    the wrecking cure, the home beetle
the same insoluble religion because son, loving
    a God of the mouthful, because gland, because
    they are obvious, because questions
spurt towards the outside.

Then I personally cried bad
checks but avoided misprision,
cast out sums from my living room
with the discovery of black,
cast out the Beloved from my bedroom
by discovering the dead
bolt. I dipped my chest
in vodka and then
terrorized myself
with lighted matches.
I said it was a game.
I said life can be rough.
I dictated the terms
of my own decapitation.
I was unable to suggest a last act.
The was was set to explode in five seconds.
Headless, heedless, horseless,
I can't say I was able to stop the timer.

LEARNING FROM LUMPINESS

In the interval of deco affection
I can't live time.
I won't shimmer.
I'm running out of things to worry over
that's why I trust dying—
it's an authentic institution.
To the dead, forever and now and then
look identical.
For the dead, there is
no looking. Guilt flows off like wallpaper.
Let us think no more of the dead
than we think of stars winking out.
Let us listen to the voice of the instant,
breathe time clear and then exhale.

THE INJURED, THE ADMIRED

The moment turned and I took my
road out on the act,
again pleasure borrowing there.
Much mouth and a horizon anybody,
that was me in those years.
I was a catastrophe waiting
for an aquarium,
waiting for a her
like night inside weeds,
like a terrace following up
a needle, feeling
the way an actor falls on
stage when the audience grunts.

WHY NOT GET A PUPPY?

You can't just turn off the oven on that certain Sunday
once a year when time jumps ahead
and believe Sadness has gotten the word.
He's announced he's in town for the summer
and though he's a time share
he's going to see you often through the week.
He feels bad you didn't invite him
to that small party after your divorce
and now it's payback.
Trips to a doctor of mental nutrition won't help
because Sadness is all vegan.
He eats nothing with a face
as a way to make up for
all the time he spends facing you.
Console yourself in the knowledge
that he won't bring his friends this time:
Madness is off to Majorca,
and Depression is in another poem,
Suicidal Tendencies got a record deal
so they won't be around.
If you could add up all the cards
you've thrown away you'd probably build
a house, at least a guest house
or a house of cards—
and he knows that,
It's why Sadness stands outside your window
tossing pebbles at the glass.
He has no bad intentions,
he wants someone to come out and play with him,
someone to roll around with in the grass.

THESE ARE WORDS ESTRANGED IN A ROW

I dream of waking inches from facts
where conservation is not that lapsed gesture
between pith, family and earth
with the sky assuming the beauty
of a corrugated box.
How I love the gilded century
all that absence glimpsed in a jar.

Spring is made trivial,
summer is trivial, hell,
not season in the world matters
when the atmosphere thins and everywhere
takes on the golden plume
of dust to dust and nothing.

I've heard it's raining
in the middle of the world
but that's an ocean displacement,
the seas, tired of the same view,
are on the move.

The desert will turn to sea and the sea,
desert, from the misplaced houses,
though I'm no Moses,
many of us will have to move.
The moths continue work
on the woolen winter suits:
too late to close the doors.

LITTLE RED NEIGHBORHOOD

Listen to the barbaric
of ten thousand schoolgirls scratching
the nude trace of red scales rising
on the arms and legs,
the principal is calling,
nurse cries out a red
raising new stigmata
on the temperamental body
the need to scratch this
no conventional somatic rash
a scratch contagious
not by blood or breath
or taint of sexual idea
scratch passing from one
subject to another in thought
beneath story with an autumn thickness
you scratch and I think about you
scratching therefore I scratch
and in this way we are not alone
and the universe continues in the scratch
of holy past, in the scratch of holy work
and we scratch the promised now
with our long God-given nails.

THE MUSEUM OF STAMMERS

This skirmish I'm in mourning
with all the good abstractions.
This morning I inspect the Beloved's knees
find me a peculiar plant
and photograph that childish ass
then abandon it and my dissections.
I speak to a group of men who lie down
with numbers and get up dirty—
something I've been meaning to do
meaning always less the sum of its parts and every other trifle I've
    discarded with age which hides before my departure though best
    served medium and never discussed with virgins in the route, it
    comes between impossible friends late for dinner and the only
    guest without a place to begin conversation running seasonal
    round here, taking up too much space it dies and is reborn and
    dies again like those extra five pounds I've been lugging since
    New Years, meaning, replaceable, embraceable, the bad-tasting
    doctor's paste as once again I'm denied membership to the sal-
    vation club and others horse their debts while my pencils are
    chiming
I dress in a meat locker,
toast the chain-link fence.
I sleep in a bird cage,
touch myself like a squirrel expired,
like a stackable washer drier.
I get my congress of shoes to declare war
on those who like the bellicose better
than the jolt. I use my very tonight.

Sing the hymn for doorstep sing the hymn
for barrel baron (not a bad career
—another message from Mom)
but for now it's a tussle,

a slap match among those who
I certainly can't place in my hand.
The minstrels are at the door again,
just a moment while I remove last night's masque
the red food dye.
Think smaller, tighter, darker.
Ignore the tinge, please
tell me if you saw me
in the window of a doggy store
with numbers got up as a French
translation of *nouvelle riche*
would you ask how much I am?
The days have seen better elms.
If I'm guilty of anything
it's outsider trading.

THE JAR OVERFLOWING WITH EMPTINESS

This morning, those in charge of details
and world vision announce
(though exact predictions are impossible
and guessing is unwise,
additionally there may be need
of paper clarifications):
all evidence points to the one,
the eternal, the only it.

Oh my aching thread—
more diagonals I can't understand.
They might as well describe mountain light
as a system marked by gelatin beans.

Later the unrelated pipe about time
brings another imperfect rupture
and I get the swimming eye.

I'm one of the unauthorized inmates
perpendicular about life.
I continue about the business
where chance favors the dog of a garish man.

Shoes up in the ease evening
I'll spend time with sandpaper and sincere shelves
working over my cocoon past.

I GLOSS THE HISTORY OF
THE HUMAN TONGUE

I have plenty experience and a pair of slacks annotating mouths
though I've never lived the rigor
of apples longing.

There will be no discussion of the parabolic lick,
the barbaric kick, the postdecadent yaw—
I'm here to document normal.

In me words go down contemptuously.
I'm against me, against invisible stairs.
I'm not good with shorter letters.

Years ahead, some may see the residue
of this occasion,
the old midpoint becoming the new midpoint.

Come let us shower.
Be well statisticians,
a voyage intermission awaits us.

DEAR IT

I've left the is beads behind
and you small without breast,
you the fourth,
you the little then,
you of the you—
no sense shoveling hair for the hairshirts
my burning immediate context fresh.
The you words
close their distance in air.
The mauve are coming
with their swatches
and history read with water.
Torsos like mine amply express
time's bitter beer.
I've become the living damn me.
Perfume never
falls into my bed.

A QUESTION FOR THE ROMANTIC LAP

a whole drop of water is contained in this drop of water
all is pause
and me, part sand, part time

the self spars
away attention from anything pure
blinks window big
breathing out the exploded summer

is is world or instability,
joy symbolized thought,
me unavoidable
my beautiful realized?
I'll make the city gesture.

if repose is at hand
and surface eyes itself,
the living, all nine of them, are air

enough convex safety
go after the generic a, the excess a, the blooming
    righteous otherwise nudist pedestrian patrician bonus
    what an a
go now (and go parenthetically)

THE OPTIONAL OF OBVIOUS

Under a Judas sky
I was invited to paint an anger
on velvet using two expressions
and a small bit of light from the left.
Later, I worked the the
into the scene. From behind
names old shapes.
In the peeling centers,
burn lessons and curls surfaced
and always I made a brighter sameness.

THE BALLAD OF SAD CURTAIN

I was baked mute
and talking interest through chicken
pass the X, the Beloved said, *give me more Y*
from the slain fell gravel
in the butter dish horse souls
marched like feverish armies
so much music in the trivial
each day a reconstituted dream
of another reconstituted dream
if we could untie things and
discuss freedom the way we break eggs
but in our revealing tangle opera resumed
dinner more sordid milk
as the Beloved gave her best high sullen
calm got abstract
and under needle lights streets purpled
the teeth spirits were blocked
from the their usual mission
our windows covered in bark
our glass grown suspicious with age
and row upon row of stolen lemons
seersucker never fit for fall
there was blood in my wrong
there was blood in my clasps
there was blood in my music
after dinner we entered a new phase of Wilson criticism
    call it post-favorable
I think her recollection circuitry was malfunctioning
but that could be the evil I waking
or the result of snow chemistry

love beautiful and me legs me hot me green me rage me time
    me continent me bell me still me night me road me
    while me wires me mother me
time finished with a snap
but I was fixed for cash

TRANSLATIONS FROM LANGUOR NOT YET SPOKEN

In an absence of because
the head just path sometimes.
The Beloved says: *Hello, Freud time*
to the me of the new endless
(much like the me of the old endless).
Between us, enough somewhere distance
for eyes to answer draft in a world of unions.
The Beloved says: *Years will still words' air*
as if after surprise,
after the preferred all,
after the two the of the busy
the Beloved mends the biology of it.
Light is thoroughly cautious.
I shiver and roofs come to ensure water's service
(predicted the coffee-pot elders).
Splinters were a clause in memory,
the Beloved's hands charms to my back.
Blossoms sort a context
each such a cargo of her will.
I'm the if problem—
The Beloved says: *Remember distant.*
I remember necessity's fog becoming geese
as the ex-muscles gather.
I remember the what gives present.
The Beloved says: *The using is need.*
I hold out my you hands to her.
I wait for the great and.
I rest in the elegant thought culture of air.
In the sees sees sees of cleared out
the Beloved says: *With get, can't makes change.*

AN ILLUSTRATED TEXT
AIMED AT ENGINEERS

The Beloved is having needles
stuck in her again while I
I'm constructing the marathon sentence:
this is the other death,
by the adjective, death by the inaction of verbs, the subjunctive, the
inability of subjects and objects to agree in any case, death by gerund, death by dangling participle, death by the present tense, death
by etymology, by the scientific binomial, the secondary variant, by
undefined run-ons, the bold-faced colon, syllabication dots
and the dead professor who,
after parsing the last few sentences,
will fail me and I've heard New York
is not as easy place.

Someone said that any one event
is nothing in the horizon of events—
unless you're the one doing the dying,
it's your burned house, your gun's
echo between buildings near the vacant lot
and some say New York is not an easy place.

time us

If one stares too closely
at a word it may stare back
because New York is not an easy place, I'm told.

I know the new cat has been showing up a lot lately but that's because he's always jumping into my lap when I'm writing and insists on burying his face in the cup of my hand. All this purring and stirring in my lap—I have to admit I like it though New York is not an easy place—for cats.

That line was what makes the next line possible
that and a vocabulary to describe
the underlying patter of life—
if there is any in New
York which is not easy for a place.

Starched parts point to somewhere material
like plastic conduits for the fleeting image
the single life has to slide along the ground.
Profound or just another door shut against
the odor of sounds?
Only death can raise the dumb object.
I read something like that somewhere
but never learned
what it means. Still it sounds
good
at a time like this with New York
an uneasy place.

Confusion is futile
doubt has many kids

The I of the moment produces a pain jacket
to speak of the death of representation
an attack on mirrors
I am made up of bits of it
I am going toward cities
I have made a mountain from a paper clip
and planted it on a map
and they say New York is not easy

Something is blowing up downstairs
and the cats are hungry
and I am hungry
and I'm covered in child ash
and flying through the natural security skies
and some say New York isn't a place for the easy.

THE GOLDEN AGE OF PEANUT BUTTER

The eternal is not a garden of grass dazzle
and night play open like
a conqueror's waltz or the gesture
of mouse owners at the empty cage.
Let us reconsider the three lessons of history:
scraps, scroll, scowl—
there is an inch in deism becoming
monotheism becoming me-ism.
From another vantage point, fall,
rise, fall. I may
have turned that around.
Too much time at the Festival
of Let's Get Blonde
Drunk. I can tell you
when the Beloved asks for skin music
lately I'm too tired.
Familiarity breeds mild swarms
but it's unsatisfactory powder
at the love cities this evening.
I've asked her to bare one
breast when she talks to me like that.
Does it help?

SHEEP WEEP

What snow, oh my darling
can you live with my bald head?
I floss every day
with air filters in the room—
still sleep disturbs my dust.
The good thing about the universe
is it gives a man a place
of religion in the senses.
and time to arrange books
the way toads fix supper.
So much for the mind.
For the rest of the organs
I gave up science.

Oh my darling my feet are flat
and my back is hairy—
is communion possible
under the dome of a latex sky?
Events prove you must not trust
the sky nor name
a sunset with colors.
Bring lead home,
show silver only moments of true panic,
look toward the golden years.
Is there one thing
that makes it all worthwhile?

Something is happening outside:
Through a field come the virgins
floating like telescopes
and then the fathers
with chest hair coifed
in the sign of the cross

and the uncles who are silent
and the brothers are not
and all the little dogs yammering
in the key of bond traders after bonus.

www.ingramcontent.com/pod-product-compliance
Lightning Source LLC
Chambersburg PA
CBHW022346040426
42449CB00006B/749